D1520108

Jesus Once Was a Little Child

written by Susan Evans McCloud

illustrated by Alexandra Bulankina

CFI · An imprint of Cedar Fort, Inc. · Springville, Utah

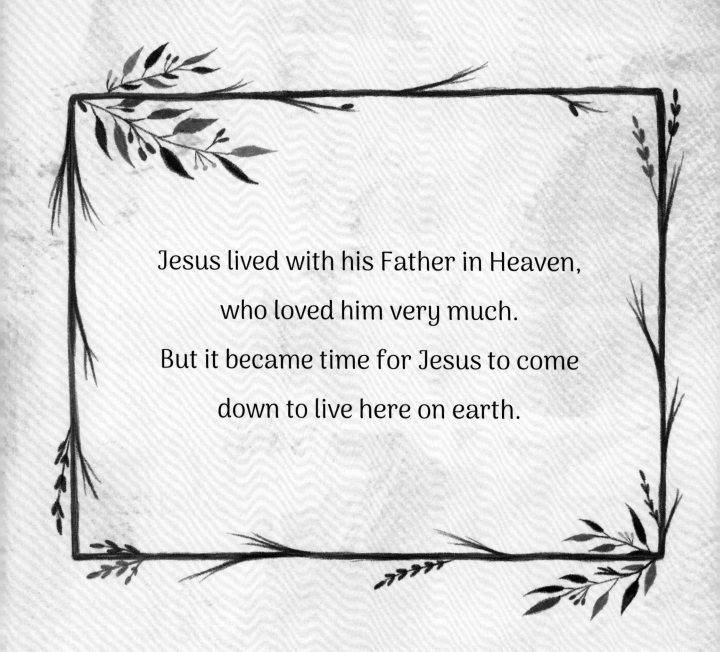

Jesus lived with his Father in Heaven,

who loved him very much.

But it became time for Jesus to come

down to live here on earth.

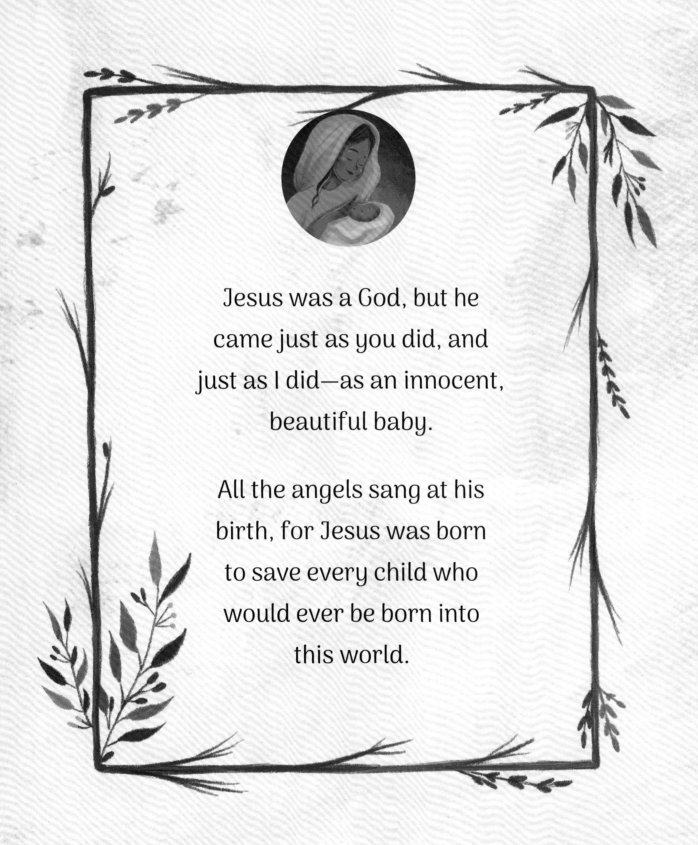

Jesus was a God, but he came just as you did, and just as I did—as an innocent, beautiful baby.

All the angels sang at his birth, for Jesus was born to save every child who would ever be born into this world.

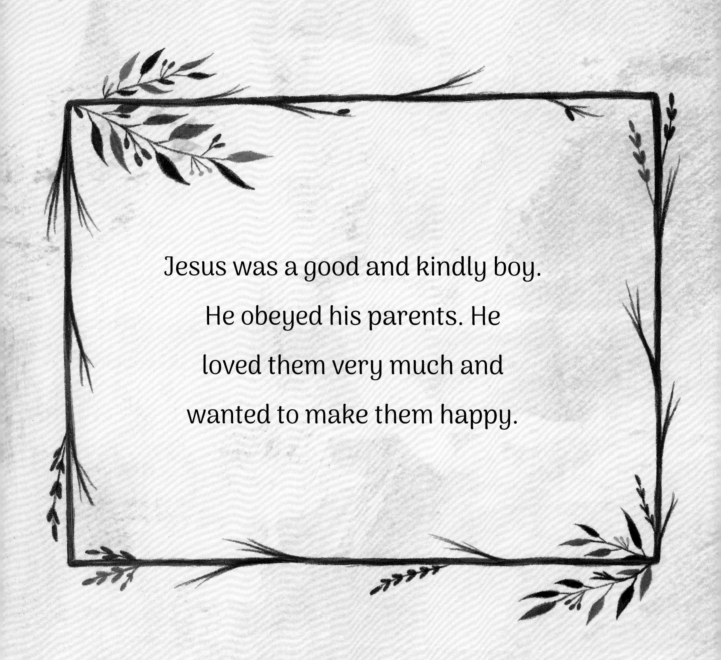

Jesus was a good and kindly boy.
He obeyed his parents. He
loved them very much and
wanted to make them happy.

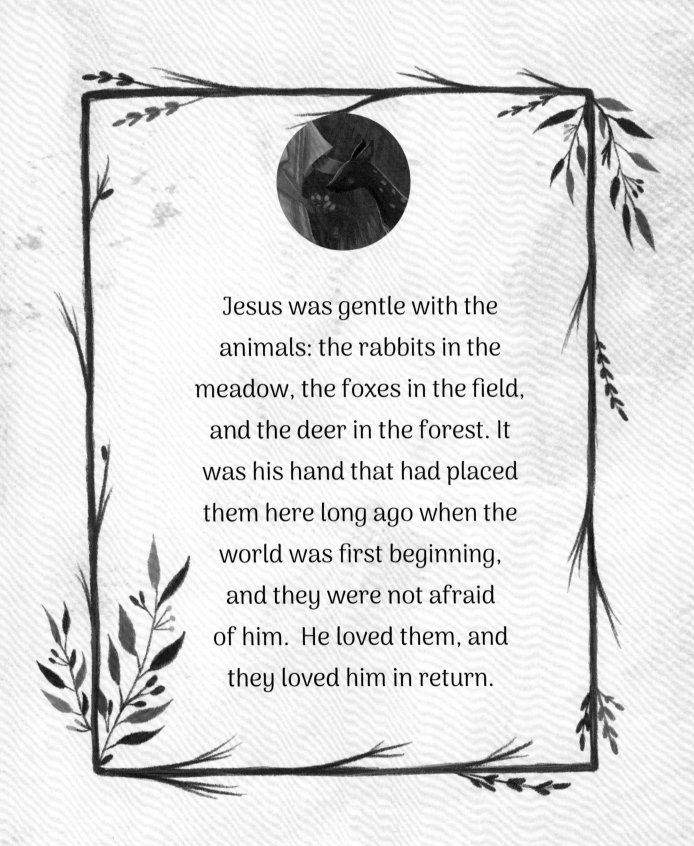

Jesus was gentle with the
animals: the rabbits in the
meadow, the foxes in the field,
and the deer in the forest. It
was his hand that had placed
them here long ago when the
world was first beginning,
and they were not afraid
of him. He loved them, and
they loved him in return.

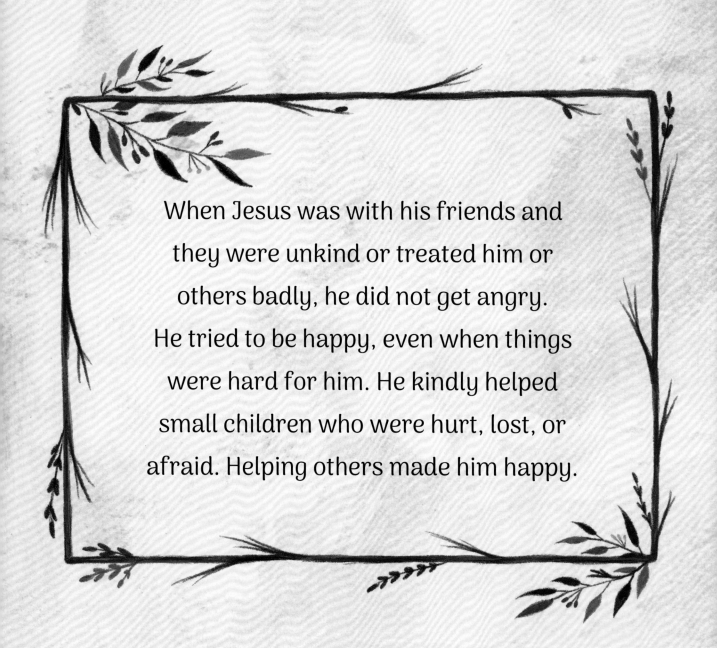

When Jesus was with his friends and
they were unkind or treated him or
others badly, he did not get angry.
He tried to be happy, even when things
were hard for him. He kindly helped
small children who were hurt, lost, or
afraid. Helping others made him happy.

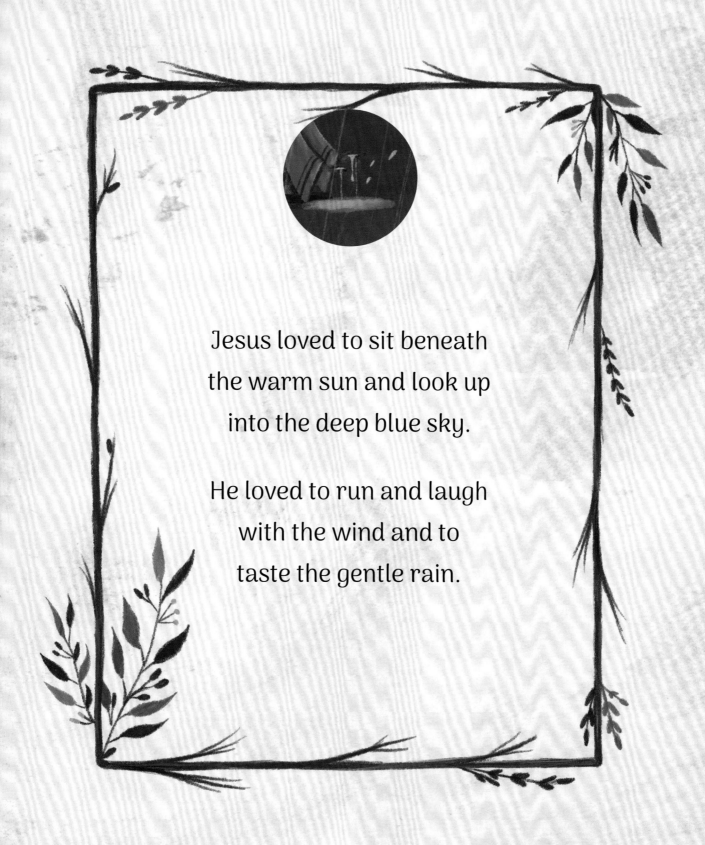

Jesus loved to sit beneath
the warm sun and look up
into the deep blue sky.

He loved to run and laugh
with the wind and to
taste the gentle rain.

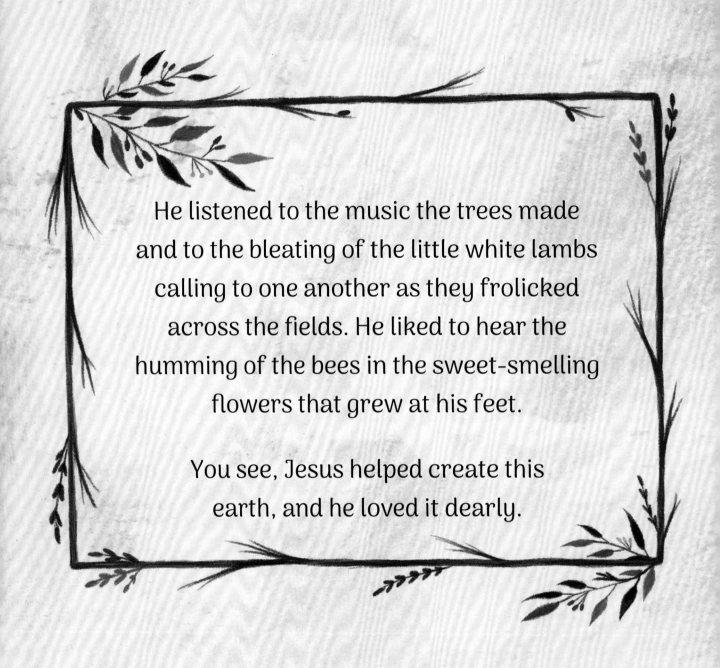

He listened to the music the trees made and to the bleating of the little white lambs calling to one another as they frolicked across the fields. He liked to hear the humming of the bees in the sweet-smelling flowers that grew at his feet.

You see, Jesus helped create this earth, and he loved it dearly.

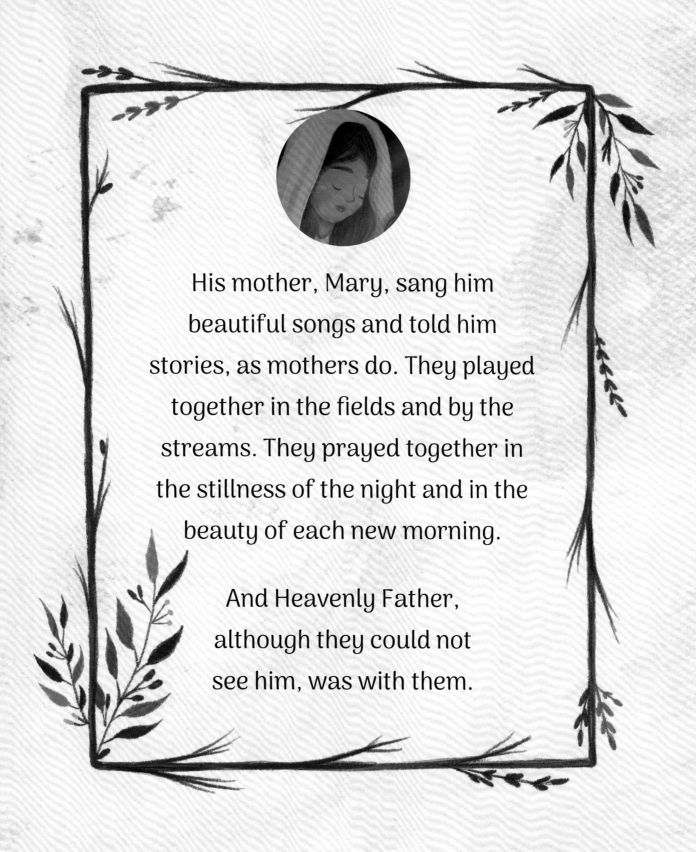

His mother, Mary, sang him beautiful songs and told him stories, as mothers do. They played together in the fields and by the streams. They prayed together in the stillness of the night and in the beauty of each new morning.

And Heavenly Father, although they could not see him, was with them.

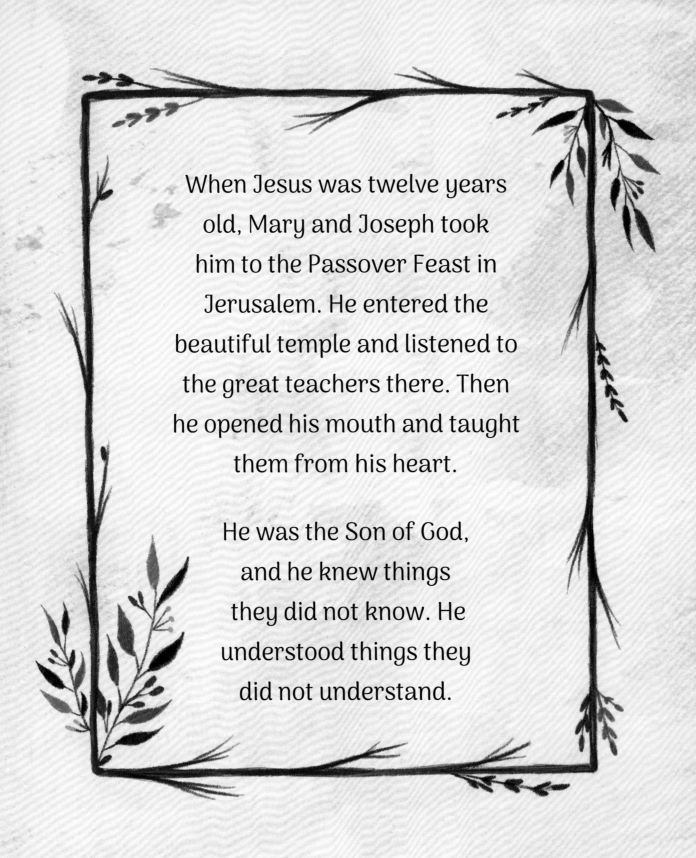

When Jesus was twelve years
old, Mary and Joseph took
him to the Passover Feast in
Jerusalem. He entered the
beautiful temple and listened to
the great teachers there. Then
he opened his mouth and taught
them from his heart.

He was the Son of God,
and he knew things
they did not know. He
understood things they
did not understand.

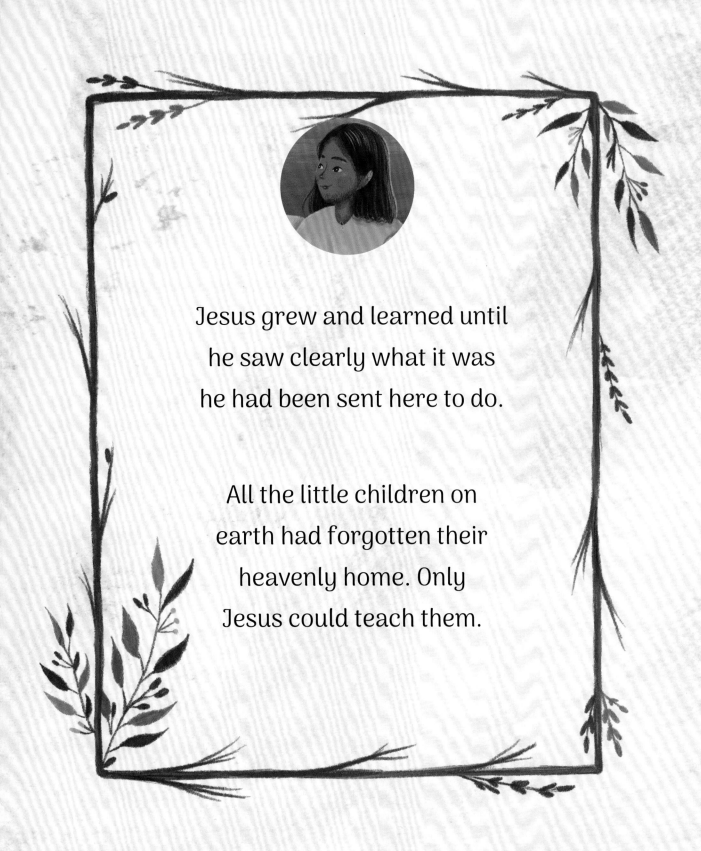

Jesus grew and learned until
he saw clearly what it was
he had been sent here to do.

All the little children on
earth had forgotten their
heavenly home. Only
Jesus could teach them.

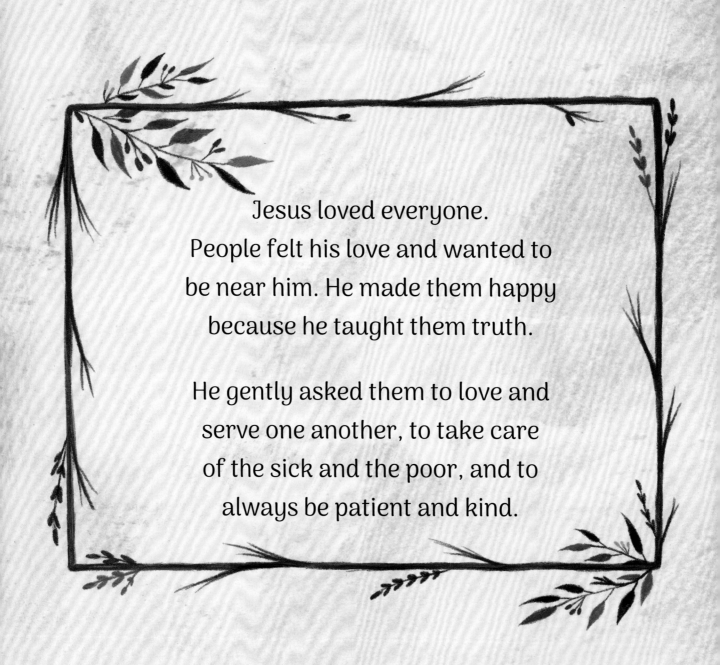

Jesus loved everyone.
People felt his love and wanted to
be near him. He made them happy
because he taught them truth.

He gently asked them to love and
serve one another, to take care
of the sick and the poor, and to
always be patient and kind.

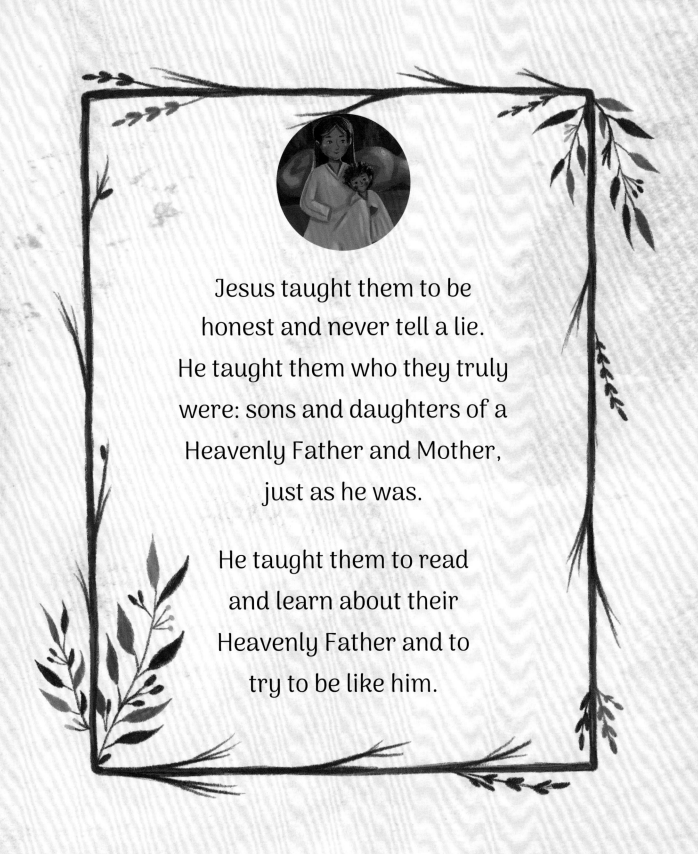

Jesus taught them to be
honest and never tell a lie.
He taught them who they truly
were: sons and daughters of a
Heavenly Father and Mother,
just as he was.

He taught them to read
and learn about their
Heavenly Father and to
try to be like him.

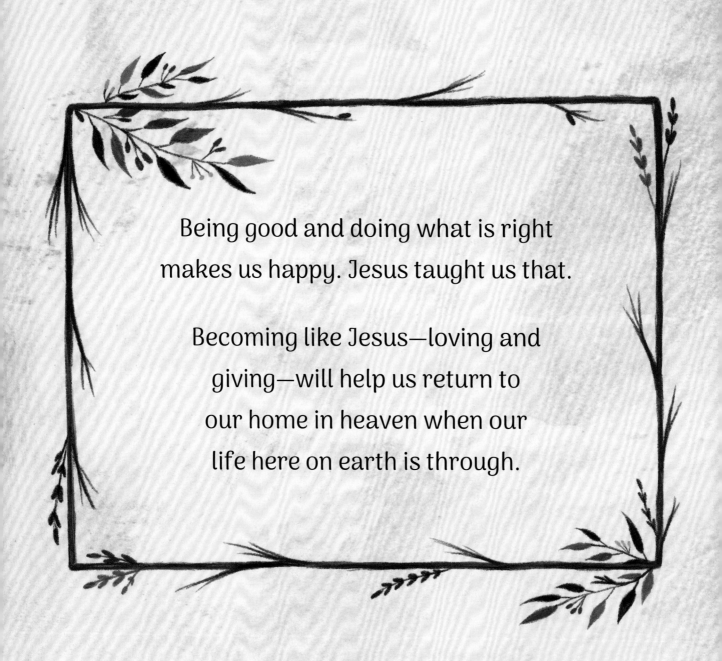

Being good and doing what is right
makes us happy. Jesus taught us that.

Becoming like Jesus—loving and
giving—will help us return to
our home in heaven when our
life here on earth is through.

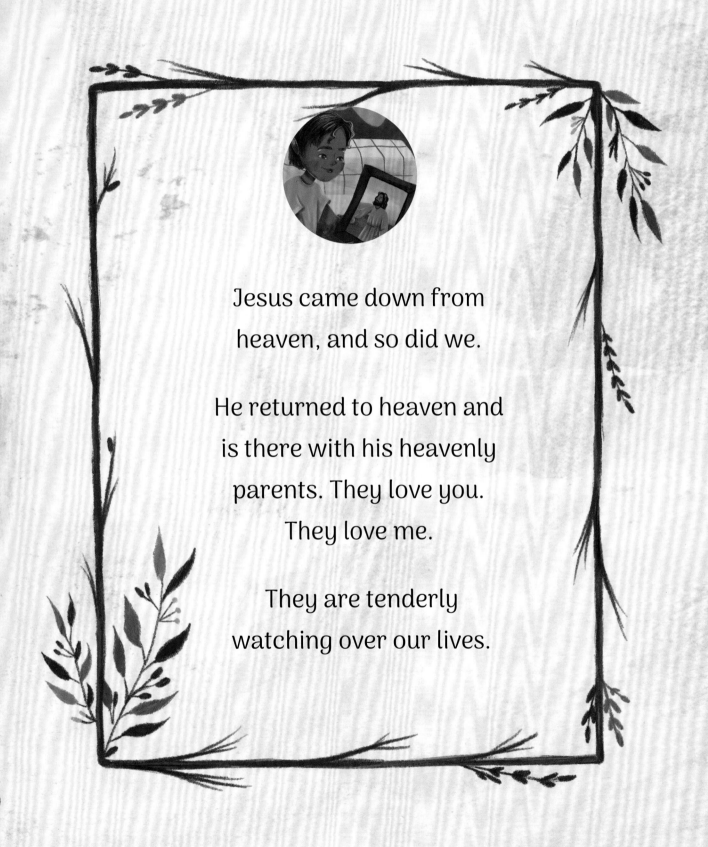

Jesus came down from
heaven, and so did we.

He returned to heaven and
is there with his heavenly
parents. They love you.
They love me.

They are tenderly
watching over our lives.

They are eagerly waiting
for us to come back to
them again someday.